MUM & Me

MUM & Me will take you on an interactive and fun journey, having a great time getting to know each other better.

Tips to enjoy MUM & Me :

- Your questions are in green. Mum's questions are in purple.

- Dip in and complete your questions in any order, whenever you want.

- Use words, drawings, doodles . . . whatever feels right for you.

- There are no right or wrong answers, just your own.

- Use the extra pages to capture anything else you would like to explore.

- Agree when and how to share your pages with the other person.

- Enjoy yourself and have fun!

A bit about Mum . . .

My full name :

My age :   Today's Date :

A picture of Mum . . . a drawing or photo

MUM

A bit about Me . . .

My full name :

My age :   Today's date :

A picture of Me . . . a drawing or photo

Me

A bit about Mum . . .

What I love watching on television :

Best films :

Top songs :

Favourite places :

Things I say a lot :

I love to eat :

MUM

A bit about Me . . .

What I love watching on television :

Best films :

Top songs :

Favourite places :

Things I say a lot :

I love to eat :

Me

Today . . .

Who I talked to :

What I did :

The best things :

The worst things :

What I wanted to do, but didn't get round to :

MUM

Today . . .

Who I talked to :

What I did :

The best things :

The worst things :

What I wanted to do, but didn't get round to :

Me

When I was younger . . .

My earliest memory :

What I was like :

When I was younger I thought that :

MUM

When I was younger . . .

My earliest memory :

What I was like :

When I was younger I thought that :

Me

Happened to me . . .

Funny things :

Embarrassing things :

Sad things :

MUM

Happened to me . . .

Funny things :

Embarrassing things :

Sad things :

Me

The way we are . . .

The ways we are similar :

The ways we are different :

Things I admire about you :

MUM

The way we are . . .

The ways we are similar :

The ways we are different :

Things I admire about you :

Me

My family . . .

Some great memories of our family :

What I love about our family :

What I would like to be different :

MUM

My family . . .

Some great memories of our family :

What I love about our family :

What I would like to be different :

Me

Family times . . .

Things I love doing with my family :

I wish we could :

I wish we didn't :

MUM

Family times . . .

Things I love doing with my family :

I wish we could :

I wish we didn't :

Me

Where I live . . .

What I remember about the places I have lived :

Things at home that are special :

Where I might like to live in the future :

MUM

Where I live . . .

What I remember about the places I have lived :

Things at home that are special :

Where I might like to live in the future :

Me

Birthdays . . .

My best memories :

How I would like to spend future birthdays :

My perfect present would be :

MUM

Birthdays . . .

My best memories :

How I would like to spend future birthdays :

My perfect present would be :

Me

Holidays . . .

My best memories :

The best places I have been :

Where I would love to visit :

MUM

Holidays . . .

My best memories :

The best places I have been :

Where I would love to visit :

Me

With friends . . .

How I feel about my friends :

What I admire most about you and your friends :

What I want to change about my friendships :

MUM

With friends . . .

How I feel about my friends :

What I admire most about you and your friends :

What I want to change about my friendships :

Me

Messages for my friends . . .

To:

To:

To:

To:

To:

To:

MUM

Messages for my friends . . .

To:

To:

To:

To:

To:

To:

Me

My spare time . . .

What I enjoy doing most in my spare time :

What I would love to do :

What I love watching you do :

MUM

My spare time . . .

What I enjoy doing most in my spare time :

What I would love to do :

What I love you watching me do :

Me

School . . .

What I loved about being at school :

What I found most difficult :

With the benefit of hindsight :

MUM

School . . .

What I love about being at school :

What I find most difficult :

My greatest learning experience :

Me

Learning . . .

What I would love to learn :

How I best like to learn :

The help I would like from you :

MUM

Learning . . .

What I would love to learn :

How I best like to learn :

The help I would like from you :

Me

Books & stories . . .

Some of my favourite books :

Books I love that I hope you will read :

Books I would love to read :

MUM

Books & stories . . .

Some of my favourite books :

Favourite characters from my books :

Books I would love to read :

Me

Some of my favourite things . . .

MUM

Some of my favourite things . . .

Me

Growing up . . .

What was exciting :

What I was concerned about :

The help and guidance I received :

MUM

Growing up . . .

What is exciting :

What I am concerned about :

The help I would like :

Me

My body . . .

How I feel about me :

What I like about me :

What I would like to share with you :

MUM

My body . . .

How I feel about me :

What I like about me :

What I would like to share with you :

Me

Being healthy . . .

A drawing of my ideas to be fit and healthy :

MUM

Being healthy . . .

A drawing of my ideas to be fit and healthy :

Me

Feeling happy . . .

The things that make me happy :

What makes me feel confident :

Who I love spending time with :

MUM

Feeling happy . . .

The things that make me happy :

What makes me feel confident :

Who I love spending time with :

Me

Feeling sad . . .

The things that make me sad :

What knocks my confidence :

What helps me when I feel sad :

MUM

Feeling sad . . .

The things that make me sad :

What knocks my confidence :

What helps me when I feel sad :

Me

My worries . . .

Things that worry me :

Some of my regrets :

How I best manage any worries :

MUM

My worries . . .

Things that worry me :

Some of my regrets :

How I best manage any worries :

Me

Falling in love . . .

My views on love :

What is important to me :

My first love and what I learnt :

MUM

Falling in love . . .

My views on love :

What is important to me :

What I have learnt so far :

Me

My future . . .

Things I want to do in my life :

Things I want to do with you :

Some words to describe the person I want to be :

MUM

My future . . .

Things I want to do in my life :

Things I want to do with you :

Some words to describe the person I want to be :

Me

My dreams . . .

What I dream about :

How I see my future :

What I wish I could spend more time doing :

MUM

My dreams . . .

What I dream about :

How I see my future :

What I wish I could spend more time doing :

Me

Mum & Me . . .

What I love about you :

What I love about us :

What I wish we could do better :

MUM

Me & Mum . . .

What I love about you :

What I love about us :

What I wish we could do better :

Me

Thoughts I have . . .

In 5 years :

I hope :

A secret :

MUM

Thoughts I have . . .

In 5 years :

I hope :

A secret :

Me

Helping others . . .

People I admire who help others :

How I like to help others :

What I could do more :

MUM

Helping others . . .

People I admire who help others :

How I like to help others :

What I could do more :

Me

Topics of Mum's choice . . .

These pages are for you, Mum, to write questions . . .

MUM

Topics of Mum's choice . . .

. . . or topics for you and your child to answer

Me

Topics of my choice . . .

These pages are for you to write questions . . .

MUM

Topics of my choice . . .

. . . or topics for you and your Mum to answer

Me

A poem about me & you . . .

MUM

A poem about me & you . . .

Me

A letter to myself based on what I
have discovered in this journal . . .

Dear Me

MUM

A letter to myself based on what I have discovered in this journal . . .

Dear Me

Me

Thinking about what I have discovered from this journal, here is a picture showing my dreams for the future . . .

MUM

Thinking about what I have discovered from this journal, here is a picture showing my dreams for the future . . .

Me

Final thoughts & doodles . . .

Final thoughts & doodles . . .

Me

MUM & me

Also available – DAD & Me

from you to me are the creators of

Gifts that touch lives ...
Gifts that preserve priceless memories and stories ...
Gifts to pass on

First published in the UK by *from you to me* April 2014
Copyright from you to me limited 2014
ISBN 978-1-907048-55-5

Printed and bound in China by Imago. This paper is manufactured from pulp sourced from forests that are legally and sustainably managed.

For more information please contact:
from you to me ltd
The Cottage Suite, The Old Brewery, 53 Wine Street, Bradford on Avon, BA15 1NS, UK

hello@fromyoutome.com
www.fromyoutome.com

Published by *from you to me* ltd

All titles are available at good gift and book shops or www.fromyoutome.com

from you to me Journals of a Lifetime
Dear Mum
Dear Dad
Dear Grandma
Dear Grandad
Dear Sister
Dear Brother
Dear Daughter
Dear Son
Dear Friend

Parent & Child
Bump to Birthday, pregnancy & first year journal
Our Story, for my daughter
Our Story, for my son
Mum to Mum – pass it on
Dear Baby, guest book

Teen & Tween
Mum & Me
Dad & Me
Rant & Rave – My School
Rant & Rave – My Holiday

Other Titles
Love Stories, anniversary & relationship journal
Cooking up Memories
Digging up Memories
Kicking off Memories
Dear Future Me
These were the Days
Christmas Present, Christmas Past

Many of these journals can be personalised online at www.fromyoutome.com

from you to me®